DISCARD

GORILLAS

New and Updated

GAIL GIBBONS

HOLIDAY HOUSE · NEW YORK

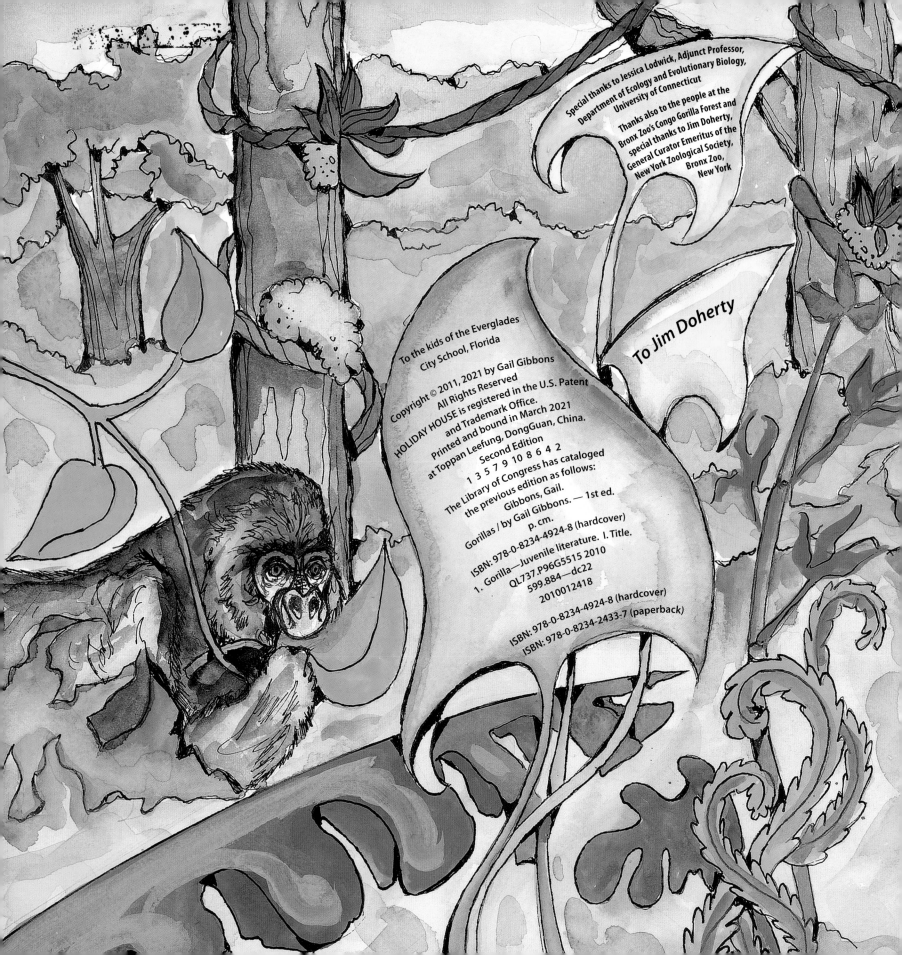

Special thanks to Jessica Lodwick, Adjunct Professor, Department of Ecology and Evolutionary Biology, University of Connecticut

Thanks also to the people at the Bronx Zoo's Congo Gorilla Forest and special thanks to Jim Doherty, General Curator Emeritus of the New York Zoological Society, Bronx Zoo, New York

To Jim Doherty

To the kids of the Everglades City School, Florida

Printed and bound in March 2021 at Toppan Leefung, DongGuan, China.
Second Edition
1 3 5 7 9 10 8 6 4 2
The Library of Congress has cataloged the previous edition as follows:
Gibbons, Gail.
Gorillas / by Gail Gibbons. — 1st ed.
p. cm.
ISBN: 978-0-8234-4924-8 (hardcover)
1. Gorilla—Juvenile literature. I. Title.
QL737.P96G5515 2010
599.884—dc22
2010012418

ISBN: 978-0-8234-4924-8 (hardcover)
ISBN: 978-0-8234-2433-7 (paperback)

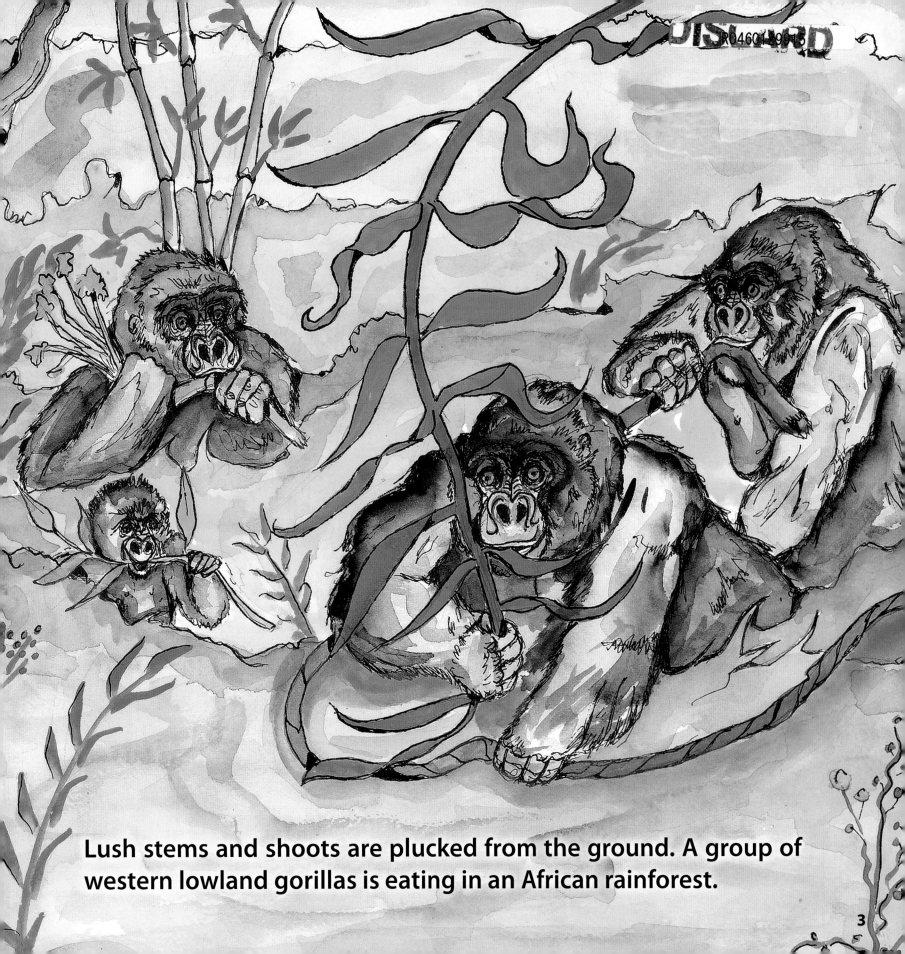

Lush stems and shoots are plucked from the ground. A group of western lowland gorillas is eating in an African rainforest.

There can be about three to thirty gorillas in a group.

All wild gorillas live in Africa. Gorillas are social animals that live in groups, sometimes called harems. A large male gorilla is in charge of the social group. This male is called a silverback.

Young adult males, called BLACKBACKS, wait for the chance to lead their own groups. They may remain in the group as long as they do not challenge the silverback.

A SILVERBACK gets his name from the hair covering his back, which has turned silver gray with age.

A group moves from place to place in search of food and safe areas to rest. The silverback sometimes takes the lead, and the other male gorillas follow. Behind them are the females with their young. At other times he keeps track of group members from the rear.

MOST WILD GORILLAS LIVE IN THE NATIONAL PARKS OF AFRICA.

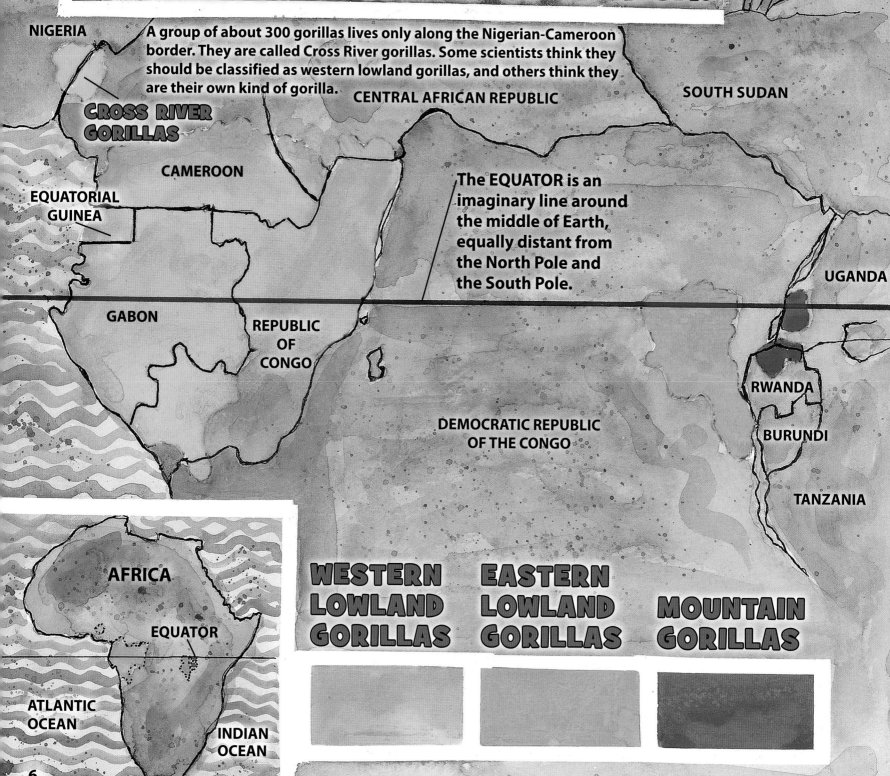

NIGERIA

A group of about 300 gorillas lives only along the Nigerian-Cameroon border. They are called Cross River gorillas. Some scientists think they should be classified as western lowland gorillas, and others think they are their own kind of gorilla.

CENTRAL AFRICAN REPUBLIC

SOUTH SUDAN

CROSS RIVER GORILLAS

CAMEROON

EQUATORIAL GUINEA

The EQUATOR is an imaginary line around the middle of Earth, equally distant from the North Pole and the South Pole.

UGANDA

GABON

REPUBLIC OF CONGO

RWANDA

DEMOCRATIC REPUBLIC OF THE CONGO

BURUNDI

TANZANIA

AFRICA

EQUATOR

ATLANTIC OCEAN

INDIAN OCEAN

WESTERN LOWLAND GORILLAS

EASTERN LOWLAND GORILLAS

MOUNTAIN GORILLAS

6

A WESTERN LOWLAND GORILLA

The smallest of the three kinds of gorillas has thick, short grayish-brown or black hair and often a patch of reddish-brown hair on its head.

AN EASTERN LOWLAND GORILLA

Larger than the western lowland gorilla, it has thick, short black hair.

The largest of the three kinds of gorillas has thick, long black hair.

A MOUNTAIN GORILLA

Most scientists think there are three kinds of gorillas. All live in African rainforests. Some gorillas live in warm, moist wooded lowland areas with swampy clearings. Other gorillas live in cold, wet, mountainous areas.

7

GORILLA CHARACTERISTICS

A MALE WESTERN LOWLAND GORILLA

Adult male gorillas are usually about 5½ feet (1.7 meters) tall. Their arms are about 4 feet (1.2 meters) long.

Adult male gorillas usually weigh between 350 and 500 pounds (160 and 225 kilograms).

They are able to grasp things with their hands and their feet.

For all gorillas, their arms are nearly twice as long as their legs.

Gorillas are big and strong.

A FEMALE WESTERN LOWLAND GORILLA

Adult female gorillas are usually about 4 feet (1.2 meters) tall. Their arms are about 3 feet (0.9 meter) long.

Adult female gorillas usually weigh about 200 pounds (90.7 kilograms).

HEAD

EAR

FOREHEAD

EYES

NOSTRILS

MOUTH

THIRTY-TWO TEETH

JAW

NECK

CHEST

ARMS

BACK

STOMACH

LEGS

Each hand has four fingers and a thumb.

FINGERNAIL

Each foot has four toes and a big toe.

Adult gorillas have no hair on their faces, their chests, the palms of their hands, or the soles of their feet. Their skin is smooth and tough.

Gorillas are smart, curious, and usually shy. But they can be scary when protecting their group.

A MOUNTAIN GORILLA

Primates are mammals that have flexible hands and feet with five digits. They include lemurs, tarsiers, monkeys, apes, and humans.

Gorillas are the largest of all primates.

10

Adult gorillas are large animals that need to eat a lot of food. Males will eat as much as 40 pounds (18.1 kilograms) of food each day. Gorillas are primarily plant eaters. Occasionally, they may eat insects, such as ants and termites.

Gorillas eat more than a hundred different kinds of plants.

BLACKBERRIES

BANANA TREE

GINGER

BAMBOO

WILD CELERY

Gorillas rarely drink water because many of the plants they eat are juicy.

Gorillas spend much of their day eating leaves, stems, shoots, roots, fruits, and seeds. Gorillas are so strong, they can easily break apart a bamboo stalk or a banana tree to eat the soft pulp inside.

The area where a group lives is called a HOME RANGE. A mountain gorilla's is usually about 7 square miles (18.1 square kilometers). A western gorilla's is usually between 7 and 9.5 square miles (18.1 to 24.6 square kilometers).

Sometimes a silverback will lead his group to the edges of his home range for special treats such as young and tender bamboo plants.

A GORILLA'S JAW AND TEETH

STRONG JAW MUSCLES

LARGE, STRONG TEETH

Gorillas stay within their home range. Much of the plant life they eat is tough, hard, and coarse. They use their powerful jaws and large teeth to strip away the toughest parts of plants and take the more tender parts for eating.

There are usually twice as many females as males in a group.

In the early morning light the silverback gets up and looks around. All is quiet. It is his responsibility to be on the alert and to protect the group. Others in the group begin to wake up.

14

The gorillas begin to move about. When they walk they almost always use their feet and the knuckles on their hands. This is called knuckle walking.

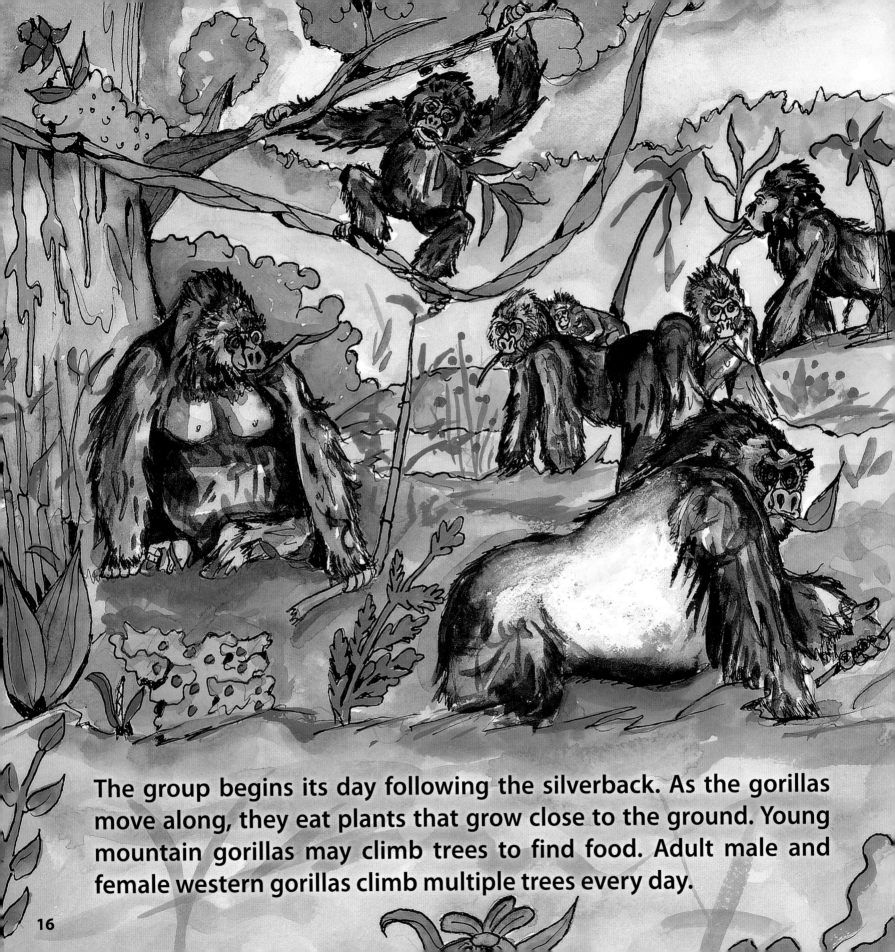

The group begins its day following the silverback. As the gorillas move along, they eat plants that grow close to the ground. Young mountain gorillas may climb trees to find food. Adult male and female western gorillas climb multiple trees every day.

Group members are peaceful and tolerant of one another. While they eat they make rumbling, purring noises and lick their lips. They also hum and sing while eating certain types of plants.

In a few hours the gorillas are full. The sun is high in the sky. It's time to allow their food to digest as they take a midday nap.

After their nap the group is active again.

Gorillas never use a nest more than once.

Young gorillas may make their nests in trees or on the ground or may sleep with their mothers.

When the day is coming to an end, the silverback chooses a safe place for the night's sleep. The silverback sits down and gathers branches and leaves around him, forming a nest. Many group members copy what he does. Throughout the night, even as he rests, the silverback is always alert.

Leopards sometimes prey on young gorillas.

Some people, called poachers, hunt gorillas.

A POACHER is someone who hunts illegally.

Another problem is that rival silverbacks from other groups or solitary males might try to attract females.

When challenged, the silverback stands up, beats his massive chest, hoots, runs, and displays his power by crashing through vegetation.

The sound of chest beating can travel over long distances, which alerts other gorillas to his strength.

He slams his hands down to the ground and CHARGES!

There is always danger.

Often, the rival male retreats and the silverback returns to his group.

HAPPY

A quiet belch, purr, hum, or laugh shows they are happy.

WORRIED

A scream or shriek shows they are worried.

ANGRY

A barking sound, or sometimes a hoot, shows they are angry.

AGGRESSIVE

A cough-grunt shows they are feeling aggressive to other group members. A loud roar shows they are feeling aggressive to an outside threat and ready to charge.

Gorillas have different ways of communicating. They use different sounds and facial expressions.

Gorillas have good vision, and they can see colors. They have good hearing and a good sense of smell too.

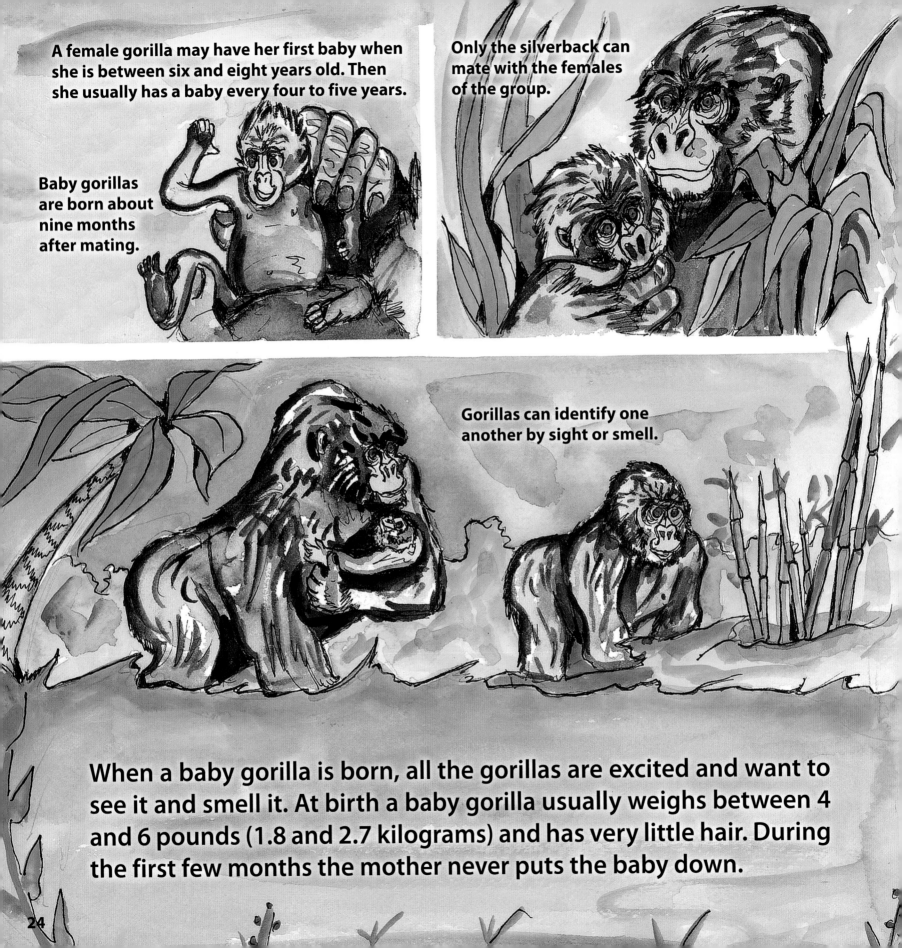

A female gorilla may have her first baby when she is between six and eight years old. Then she usually has a baby every four to five years.

Baby gorillas are born about nine months after mating.

Only the silverback can mate with the females of the group.

Gorillas can identify one another by sight or smell.

When a baby gorilla is born, all the gorillas are excited and want to see it and smell it. At birth a baby gorilla usually weighs between 4 and 6 pounds (1.8 and 2.7 kilograms) and has very little hair. During the first few months the mother never puts the baby down.

After that the baby continues to nurse and is often carried by the mother for the next three years or so. A baby gorilla has a powerful grip. It clings tightly to the hair on its mother's stomach. When it gets older, it rides on her back.

After six months the young gorilla has learned to walk. A few months later, it plays with other young gorillas whenever the adults rest. Play helps young gorillas gain strength and skills they will need all their lives.

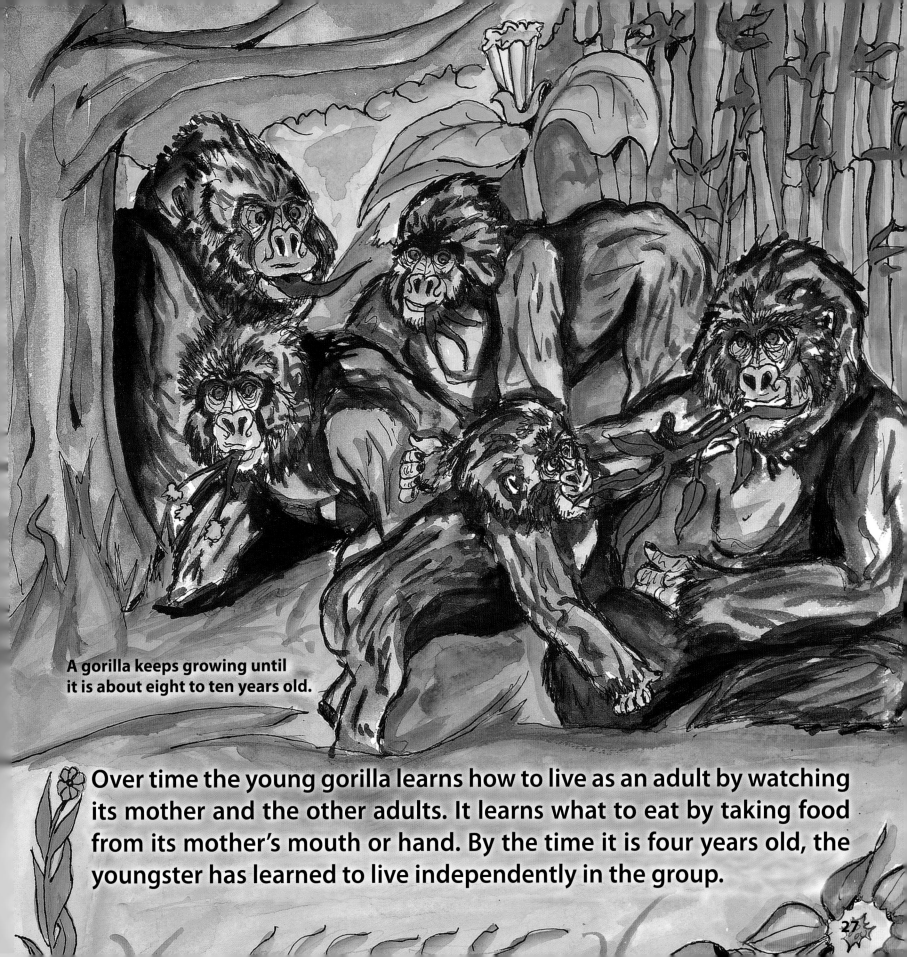

A gorilla keeps growing until
it is about eight to ten years old.

Over time the young gorilla learns how to live as an adult by watching its mother and the other adults. It learns what to eat by taking food from its mother's mouth or hand. By the time it is four years old, the youngster has learned to live independently in the group.

Logging, mining, and farming destroy huge areas of the rainforests where gorillas live. They are also hunted.

All wild gorillas are endangered. People are their worst enemy.

There are guided tours to educate people about the need to protect gorillas in their natural environment.

Reserves have been set aside to protect gorillas. Rangers and conservation workers oversee these areas.

Only western lowland gorillas are in zoos. Eastern lowland gorillas and mountain gorillas are very rare, and scientists believe they should be left in the wild.

Zoos have helped people learn to respect gorillas and understand why they should be protected.

EASTERN
LOWLAND
GORILLAS

Gorillas are peaceful and intelligent. They should be allowed to continue to live in the wild places where they have lived for millions of years.

MORE ABOUT GORILLAS . . .

In 1925 the Virunga Mountains National Park was established in the rainforests of Africa to protect mountain gorillas. This was the first national park in Africa. Today it is larger and is called the Virunga National Park.

In the 1950s an American named George Schaller became the first scientist to study mountain gorillas in the wild.

Dian Fossey, an American zoologist, lived among mountain gorillas between 1966 and 1985. Her curiosity and interaction with them provided new information about gorillas.

It is believed that about 100,000 western lowland gorillas, 4,000 eastern lowland gorillas, and fewer than about 1,000 mountain gorillas are living in Africa today.

There are about 350 gorillas that live in the zoos of the United States and Canada. They are all western lowland gorillas.

Sometimes a mother gorilla gives birth to twins. Gorillas can live to be about thirty-five years old in the wild and to about fifty years old in zoos.

The Bronx Zoo in New York has the world's largest manmade African rainforest for gorillas. About twenty-five gorillas live in its Congo Gorilla Forest.

In 1972 Dr. Francine Patterson, known as Penny, began teaching a young gorilla sign language. The gorilla, Koko, appeared to understand the meaning of more than two thousand words.

The chest of an adult male mountain gorilla is massive. It can be larger than 4 feet (1.2 meters) around. There are special air sacs within their chest that makes their chest beat sound loud and impressive.

WEBSITES

African Wildlife Foundation
www.awf.org
The Gorilla Foundation
www.gorilla.org
The Bronx Zoo
www.bronxzoo.com
The Toronto Zoo
www.torontozoo.com